This book belongs to:

....

....

....

Page	Title	Author
1		
2		
3		
4		
5		
6		
7		
8		
9		
10		
11		
12		
13		
14		
15		
16		
17		
18		
19		
20		
21		
22		
23		
24		
25		

Page	Title	Author
26		
27		
28		
29		
30		
31		
32		
33		
34		
35		
36		
37		
38		
39		
40		
41		
42		
43		
44		
45		
46		
47		
48		
49		
50		

Page	Title	Author
51		
52		
53		
54		
55		
56		
57		
58		
59		
60		
61		
62		
63		
64		
65		
66		
67		
68		
69		
70		
71		
72		
73		
74		
75		

Page	Title	Author
76		
77		
78		
79		
80		
81		
82		
83		
84		
85		
86		
87		
88		
89		
90		
91		
92		
93		
94		
95		
96		
97		
98		
99		
100		

1

Started:

....

Finished:

....

Source:

....

Why i read it:

....
....
....

It inspired me to:

....
....
....

Rating:

1 2 3 4 5

Ease of reading

1 2 3 4 5

🙁 😐 🙂

Title:

Author: ....

Subject: .... **Genre:** ....

Page count: .... **Pub date:** ....

Poperback ☐   e-book ☐   audiobook ☐

Fiction ☐   non fiction ☐

My review: ....
....
....
....
....
....
....
....
....
....
....
....
....
....
....
....

Quote from this book:

Title:

Author: ....

Subject: .... Genre: ....

Page count: .... Pub date: ....

Poperback ☐   e-book ☐   audiobook ☐

Fiction ☐   non fiction ☐

My review: ....
....
....
....
....
....
....
....
....
....
....
....
....
....
....
....

Quote from this book:

Started:

....

Finished:

....

Source:

....

Why i read it:

....
....
....

It inspired me to:

....
....
....

Rating:

1   2   3   4   5

Ease of reading

1   2   3   4   5

☹   😐   🙂

3

Started:

Finished:

Source:

Why i read it:

It inspired me to:

Rating:

1 2 3 4 5

Ease of reading

1 2 3 4 5

Title:

Author:

Subject: Genre:

Page count: Pub date:

Poperback ☐   e-book ☐   audiobook ☐

Fiction ☐   non fiction ☐

My review:

Quote from this book:

Title:

4

Author: ....

Subject: .... Genre: ....

Page count: .... Pub date: ....

Paperback ☐   e-book ☐   audiobook ☐

Fiction ☐   non fiction ☐

My review: ....
....
....
....
....
....
....
....
....
....
....
....
....
....

Quote from this book:

Started:

....

Finished:

....

Source:

....

Why i read it:
....
....
....

It inspired me to:
....
....
....

Rating:

1 2 3 4 5

Ease of reading

1 2 3 4 5

☹ 😐 🙂

5

Started:

Finished:

Source:

Why i read it:

It inspired me to:

Rating:

1 2 3 4 5

Ease of reading

1 2 3 4 5

😦 😐 😊

Title:

Author:

Subject: Genre:

Page count: Pub date:

Poperback ☐   e-book ☐   audiobook ☐

Fiction ☐   non fiction ☐

My review:

Quote from this book:

Title:

6

Author: ....

Subject: .... Genre: ....

Page count: .... Pub date: ....

Poperback ☐   e-book ☐   audiobook ☐

Fiction ☐   non fiction ☐

Started:

....

Finished:

....

Source:

....

My review: ....
....
....
....
....
....
....
....
....
....
....
....
....
....

Why i read it:

....
....
....

It inspired me to:

....
....
....

Rating:

1   2   3   4   5

Ease of reading

1   2   3   4   5

☹   😐   🙂

Quote from this book:

7

Started:

....

Finished:

....

Source:

....

Why i read it:

....
....
....

It inspired me to:

....
....
....

Rating:

1 2 3 4 5

Ease of reading

1 2 3 4 5

☹ 😐 🙂

Title:

Author: ....

Subject: .... **Genre:** ....

Page count: .... **Pub date:** ....

Poperback ☐   e-book ☐   audiobook ☐

Fiction ☐   non fiction ☐

My review: ....
....
....
....
....
....
....
....
....
....
....
....
....
....
....
....

Quote from this book:

Title:

8

Author: ....

Subject: .... Genre: ....

Page count: .... Pub date: ....

Poperback ☐   e-book ☐   audiobook ☐

Fiction ☐   non fiction ☐

My review: ....
....
....
....
....
....
....
....
....
....
....
....
....
....

Quote from this book:

Started:
....

Finished:
....

Source:
....

Why i read it.
....
....
....

It inspired me to:
....
....
....

Rating:

1 2 3 4 5

Ease of reading

1 2 3 4 5

☹ 😐 🙂

9

Started:
....

Finished:
....

Source:
....

Why i read it:
....
....
....

It inspired me to:
....
....
....

Rating:

1 2 3 4 5

Ease of reading

1 2 3 4 5

☹ 😐 🙂

Title:

Author: ....

Subject: .... **Genre:** ....

Page count: .... **Pub date:** ....

Poperback ☐   e-book ☐   audiobook ☐

Fiction ☐   non fiction ☐

My review: ....
....
....
....
....
....
....
....
....
....
....
....
....
....
....
....
....

Quote from this book:

Title:

Author: ....

Subject: .... Genre: ....

Page count: .... Pub date: ....

Poperback ☐   e-book ☐   audiobook ☐

Fiction ☐   non fiction ☐

My review: ....
....
....
....
....
....
....
....
....
....
....
....
....
....

Quote from this book:

Started:
....
Finished:
....
Source:
....

Why i read it.
....
....

It inspired me to:
....
....
....

Rating:

1 2 3 4 5

Ease of reading

1 2 3 4 5

☹ 😐 🙂

11

Started:

....

Finished:

....

Source:

....

Why i read it:

....
....
....

It inspired me to:

....
....
....

Rating:

1 2 3 4 5

Ease of reading

1 2 3 4 5

☹ 😐 🙂

Title:

Author: ....

Subject: .... **Genre:** ....

Page count: .... **Pub date:** ....

Poperback ☐   e-book ☐   audiobook ☐

Fiction ☐   non fiction ☐

My review: ....
....
....
....
....
....
....
....
....
....
....
....
....
....
....
....

Quote from this book:

Title:

12

Author: ....

Subject: .... Genre: ....

Page count: .... Pub date: ....

Poperback ☐   e-book ☐   audiobook ☐

Fiction ☐   non fiction ☐

My review: ....
....
....
....
....
....
....
....
....
....
....
....
....
....
....

Quote from this book:

Started:

....

Finished:

....

Source:

....

Why i read it:
....
....
....

It inspired me to:
....
....
....

Rating:

1   2   3   4   5

Ease of reading

1   2   3   4   5

☹   😐   🙂

13

Title:

Started:

Finished:

Source:

Why i read it:

It inspired me to:

Rating:

1 2 3 4 5

Ease of reading

1 2 3 4 5

Author: ....

Subject: .... Genre: ....

Page count: .... Pub date: ....

Poperback ☐   e-book ☐   audiobook ☐

Fiction ☐   non fiction ☐

My review: ....
....
....
....
....
....
....
....
....
....
....
....
....
....
....
....
....

Quote from this book:

Title:

Author: ....

Subject:.......................... Genre: ....

Page count: .... Pub date: ....

Poperback ☐   e-book ☐   audiobook ☐

Fiction ☐   non fiction ☐

My review:..
....
....
....
....
....
....
....
....
....
....
....
....
....
....

Quote from this book:

Started:

....

Finished:

....

Source:

....

Why i read it:
....
....
....

It inspired me to:
....
....
....

Rating:

1   2   3   4   5

Ease of reading

1   2   3   4   5

☹   😐   🙂

15

Started:

....

Finished:

....

Source:

....

Why i read it:

....
....
....

It inspired me to:

....
....
....

Rating:

1 2 3 4 5

Ease of reading

1 2 3 4 5

🙁   😐   🙂

Title:

Author: ....

Subject: .... **Genre:** ....

Page count: .... **Pub date:** ....

Poperback ☐   e-book ☐   audiobook ☐

Fiction ☐   non fiction ☐

My review: ....
....
....
....
....
....
....
....
....
....
....
....
....
....
....
....
....

Quote from this book:

Title:

16

Author: ....

Subject: .... Genre: ....

Page count: .... Pub date: ....

Poperback ☐   e-book ☐   audiobook ☐

Fiction ☐   non fiction ☐

Started:

....

Finished:

....

Source:

....

My review: ....
....
....
....
....
....
....
....
....
....
....
....
....
....
....
....

Why i read it.

....
....
....

It inspired me to:

....
....
....

Quote from this book:

Rating:

1   2   3   4   5

Ease of reading

1   2   3   4   5

☹   😐   🙂

17

Started:
....

Finished:
....

Source:

....

Why i read it:
....
....
....

It inspired me to:
....
....
....

Rating:

1 2 3 4 5

Ease of reading

1 2 3 4 5

☹ 😐 🙂

Title:

Author: ....

Subject: .... **Genre:** ....

Page count: .... **Pub date:** ....

Poperback ☐   e-book ☐   audiobook ☐

Fiction ☐   non fiction ☐

My review: ....
....
....
....
....
....
....
....
....
....
....
....
....
....
....

Quote from this book:

Title:

18

Author: ....

Subject: .... Genre: ....

Page count: .... Pub date: ....

Poperback ☐   e-book ☐   audiobook ☐
        Fiction ☐   non fiction ☐

My review: ....
....
....
....
....
....
....
....
....
....
....
....
....
....

Quote from this book:

Started:
....

Finished:
....

Source:
....

Why i read it:
....
....
....

It inspired me to:
....
....
....

Rating:

1   2   3   4   5

Ease of reading

1   2   3   4   5

☹   😐   🙂

19

Started:

....

Finished:

....

Source:

....

Why i read it:

....
....
....

It inspired me to:

....
....
....

Rating:

1   2   3   4   5

Ease of reading

1   2   3   4   5

😟   😐   🙂

Title:

Author: ....

Subject: .... **Genre:** ....

Page count: .... **Pub date:** ....

Poperback ☐   e-book ☐   audiobook ☐

Fiction ☐   non fiction ☐

My review: ....
....
....
....
....
....
....
....
....
....
....
....
....
....
....
....
....

Quote from this book:

Title:

20

Author: ....

Subject: .... Genre: ....

Page count: .... Pub date: ....

Poperback ☐   e-book ☐   audiobook ☐

Fiction ☐   non fiction ☐

My review: ....
....
....
....
....
....
....
....
....
....
....
....
....
....
....
....

Quote from this book:

Started:

....

Finished:

....

Source:

....

Why i read it:
....
....

It inspired me to:
....
....
....

Rating:

1   2   3   4   5

Ease of reading

1   2   3   4   5

😟   😐   😊

21

Started:

....

Finished:

....

Source:

....

Why i read it:

....
....
....

It inspired me to:

....
....
....

Rating:

1 2 3 4 5

Ease of reading

1 2 3 4 5

☹ 😐 🙂

Title:

Author: ....

Subject: .... **Genre:** ....

Page count: .... **Pub date:** ....

Paperback ☐   e-book ☐   audiobook ☐

Fiction ☐   non fiction ☐

My review: ....
....
....
....
....
....
....
....
....
....
....
....
....
....
....
....
....
....

Quote from this book:

Title:

22

Author: ....

Subject: .... Genre: ....

Page count: .... Pub date: ....

Poperback ☐   e-book ☐   audiobook ☐

Fiction ☐   non fiction ☐

My review: ....
....
....
....
....
....
....
....
....
....
....
....
....
....
....

Quote from this book:

Started:
....

Finished:
....

Source:
....

Why i read it:
....
....
....

It inspired me to:
....
....
....

Rating:

1 2 3 4 5

Ease of reading

1 2 3 4 5

☹ 😐 🙂

23

Started:

....

Finished:

....

Source:

....

Why i read it:

....
....
....

It inspired me to:

....
....
....

Rating:

1 2 3 4 5

Ease of reading

1 2 3 4 5

☹ 😐 🙂

Title:

Author: ....

Subject: .... **Genre:** ....

Page count: .... **Pub date:** ....

Poperback ☐   e-book ☐   audiobook ☐

Fiction ☐   non fiction ☐

My review: ....
....
....
....
....
....
....
....
....
....
....
....
....
....
....
....

Quote from this book:

Title:

24

Author: ....

Subject: .... Genre: ....

Page count: .... Pub date: ....

Poperback ☐   e-book ☐   audiobook ☐

Fiction ☐   non fiction ☐

My review: ....
....
....
....
....
....
....
....
....
....
....
....
....
....
....
....

Quote from this book:

Started:

....

Finished:

....

Source:

....

Why i read it:

....
....
....

It inspired me to:

....
....
....

Rating:

1 2 3 4 5

Ease of reading

1 2 3 4 5

☹ 😐 🙂

25

Started:

....

Finished:

....

Source:

....

Why i read it:

....
....
....

It inspired me to:

....
....
....

Rating:

1   2   3   4   5

Ease of reading

1   2   3   4   5

😞   😐   😊

Title:

Author: ....

Subject: .... **Genre:** ....

Page count: .... **Pub date:** ....

Poperback ☐   e-book ☐   audiobook ☐

Fiction ☐   non fiction ☐

My review: ....
....
....
....
....
....
....
....
....
....
....
....
....
....
....
....

Quote from this book:

Title:

26

Author: ....

Subject: .... Genre: ....

Page count: .... Pub date: ....

Poperback ☐   e-book ☐   audiobook ☐

Fiction ☐   non fiction ☐

My review: ....
....
....
....
....
....
....
....
....
....
....
....
....
....
....

Quote from this book:

Started:

....

Finished:

....

Source:

....

Why i read it:
....
....
....

It inspired me to:
....
....
....

Rating:

1 2 3 4 5

Ease of reading

1 2 3 4 5

☹ 😐 🙂

27

Started:

....

Finished:

....

Source:

....

Why i read it:

....
....
....

It inspired me to:

....
....
....

Rating:

1 2 3 4 5

Ease of reading

1 2 3 4 5

☹ 😐 🙂

Title:

Author: ....

Subject: .... Genre: ....

Page count: .... Pub date: ....

Poperback ☐   e-book ☐   audiobook ☐

Fiction ☐   non fiction ☐

My review: ....
....
....
....
....
....
....
....
....
....
....
....
....
....
....
....

Quote from this book:

Title:

28

Author: ....

Subject: .... Genre: ....

Page count: .... Pub date: ....

Poperback ☐   e-book ☐   audiobook ☐

Fiction ☐   non fiction ☐

My review: ....
....
....
....
....
....
....
....
....
....
....
....
....
....
....

Quote from this book:

Started:

....

Finished:

....

Source:

....

Why i read it:

....
....

It inspired me to:

....
....
....

Rating:

1 2 3 4 5

Ease of reading

1 2 3 4 5

☹ 😐 🙂

29

Started:

....

Finished:

....

Source:

....

Why i read it:

....
....
....

It inspired me to:

....
....
....

Rating:

1 2 3 4 5

Ease of reading

1 2 3 4 5

😞   😐   🙂

Title:

Author: ....

Subject: .... **Genre:** ....

Page count: .... **Pub date:** ....

Poperback ☐   e-book ☐   audiobook ☐

Fiction ☐   non fiction ☐

My review: ....
....
....
....
....
....
....
....
....
....
....
....
....
....
....
....
....
....

Quote from this book:

Title:

Author: ....

Subject: .... Genre: ....

Page count: .... Pub date: ....

Paperback ☐   e-book ☐   audiobook ☐

Fiction ☐   non fiction ☐

Started:

....

Finished:

....

Source:

....

My review: ....
....
....
....
....
....
....
....
....
....
....
....
....

Why i read it:

....
....
....

It inspired me to:

....
....
....

Rating:

1   2   3   4   5

Ease of reading

1   2   3   4   5

☹   😐   🙂

Quote from this book:

31

Title:

Started:

Finished:

Source:

Author: ....

Subject: .... Genre: ....

Page count: .... Pub date: ....

Poperback ☐   e-book ☐   audiobook ☐

Fiction ☐   non fiction ☐

Why i read it:
....
....
....

It inspired me to:
....
....
....

My review: ....
....
....
....
....
....
....
....
....
....
....
....
....
....
....

Rating:

1 2 3 4 5

Ease of reading

1 2 3 4 5

☹ 😐 🙂

Quote from this book:

Title:

Author: ....

Subject: .... Genre: ....

Page count: .... Pub date: ....

Paperback ☐   e-book ☐   audiobook ☐

Fiction ☐   non fiction ☐

My review: ....
....
....
....
....
....
....
....
....
....
....
....
....
....
....

Quote from this book:

Started:

....

Finished:

....

Source:

....

Why i read it:
....
....
....

It inspired me to:
....
....
....

Rating:

1   2   3   4   5

Ease of reading

1   2   3   4   5

☹   😐   🙂

33

Title:

Started:

Finished:

Source:

Why i read it:

It inspired me to:

Rating:

1 2 3 4 5

Ease of reading

1 2 3 4 5

Author: ....

Subject: .... **Genre:** ....

Page count: .... **Pub date:** ....

Poperback ☐   e-book ☐   audiobook ☐

Fiction ☐   non fiction ☐

My review: ....
....
....
....
....
....
....
....
....
....
....
....
....
....
....
....
....

Quote from this book:

Title:

Author: ....

Subject: .... Genre: ....

Page count: .... Pub date: ....

Poperback ☐   e-book ☐   audiobook ☐

Fiction ☐   non fiction ☐

Started:

....

Finished:

....

Source:

....

My review: ....

....

....

....

....

....

....

....

....

....

....

....

....

....

Why i read it:

....

....

....

It inspired me to:

....

....

....

Rating:

1   2   3   4   5

Ease of reading

1   2   3   4   5

☹   😐   🙂

Quote from this book:

35

Title:

Started:

Finished:

Source:

Author: ....

Subject: .... **Genre:** ....

Page count: .... **Pub date:** ....

Poperback ☐   e-book ☐   audiobook ☐

Fiction ☐   non fiction ☐

Why i read it:
....
....
....

It inspired me to:
....
....
....

Rating:

1 2 3 4 5

Ease of reading

1 2 3 4 5

☹ 😐 🙂

My review: ....
....
....
....
....
....
....
....
....
....
....
....
....
....
....

Quote from this book:

Title:

36

Author: ....

Subject: .... Genre: ....

Page count: .... Pub date: ....

Poperback ☐   e-book ☐   audiobook ☐

Fiction ☐   non fiction ☐

My review: ....
....
....
....
....
....
....
....
....
....
....
....
....
....
....

Quote from this book:

Started:

....

Finished:

....

Source:

....

Why i read it:
....
....
....

It inspired me to:
....
....
....

Rating:

1 2 3 4 5

Ease of reading

1 2 3 4 5

☹️ 😐 🙂

37

Title:

Started:

Finished:

Source:

Author: ....

Subject: .... Genre: ....

Page count: .... Pub date: ....

Poperback ☐   e-book ☐   audiobook ☐

Fiction ☐   non fiction ☐

Why i read it:
....
....
....

My review: ....
....
....
....
....
....
....
....
....
....

It inspired me to:
....
....
....

....
....
....
....
....
....
....

Rating:

1   2   3   4   5

Ease of reading

1   2   3   4   5

☹   😐   🙂

Quote from this book:

Title:

Author: ....

Subject: .... Genre: ....

Page count: .... Pub date: ....

Poperback ☐   e-book ☐   audiobook ☐

Fiction ☐   non fiction ☐

My review: ....
....
....
....
....
....
....
....
....
....
....
....
....
....
....
....

Quote from this book:

Started:
....

Finished:
....

Source:
....

Why i read it:
....
....
....

It inspired me to:
....
....
....

Rating:

1 2 3 4 5

Ease of reading

1 2 3 4 5

😞 😐 🙂

39

Started:

....

Finished:

....

Source:

....

Why i read it:

....
....
....

It inspired me to:

....
....
....

Rating:

1 2 3 4 5

Ease of reading

1 2 3 4 5

☹ 😐 🙂

Title:

Author: ....

Subject: .... **Genre:** ....

Page count: .... **Pub date:** ....

Poperback ☐   e-book ☐   audiobook ☐

Fiction ☐   non fiction ☐

My review: ....
....
....
....
....
....
....
....
....
....
....
....
....
....
....
....
....

Quote from this book:

Title:

40

Author: ....

Subject: .... Genre: ....

Page count: .... Pub date: ....

Poperback ☐   e-book ☐   audiobook ☐

Fiction ☐   non fiction ☐

My review: ....
....
....
....
....
....
....
....
....
....
....
....
....
....

Quote from this book:

Started:
....

Finished:
....

Source:
....

Why i read it:
....
....
....

It inspired me to:
....
....
....

Rating:

1 2 3 4 5

Ease of reading

1 2 3 4 5

☹ 😐 🙂

41

Started:

....

Finished:

....

Source:

....

Why i read it:

....
....
....

It inspired me to:

....
....
....

Rating:

1 2 3 4 5

Ease of reading

1 2 3 4 5

☹ 😐 🙂

Title:

Author: ....

Subject: .... **Genre:** ....

Page count: .... **Pub date:** ....

Poperback ☐   e-book ☐   audiobook ☐

Fiction ☐   non fiction ☐

My review: ....
....
....
....
....
....
....
....
....
....
....
....
....
....
....
....

Quote from this book:

Title:

42

Author: ....

Subject: .... Genre: ....

Page count: .... Pub date: ....

Poperback ☐   e-book ☐   audiobook ☐

Fiction ☐   non fiction ☐

My review: ....
....
....
....
....
....
....
....
....
....
....
....
....
....
....

Quote from this book:

Started:
....

Finished:
....

Source:

....

Why i read it:
....
....
....

It inspired me to:
....
....
....

Rating:

1 2 3 4 5

Ease of reading

1 2 3 4 5

☹ 😐 🙂

43

Title:

Started:

Finished:

Source:

Why i read it:

It inspired me to:

Rating:

1 2 3 4 5

Ease of reading

1 2 3 4 5

Author:

Subject: Genre:

Page count: Pub date:

Poperback ☐   e-book ☐   audiobook ☐

Fiction ☐   non fiction ☐

My review:

Quote from this book:

Title:

44

Author: ....

Subject: .... Genre: ....

Page count: .... Pub date: ....

Poperback ☐   e-book ☐   audiobook ☐

Fiction ☐   non fiction ☐

My review: ....
....
....
....
....
....
....
....
....
....
....
....
....
....
....
....

Quote from this book:

Started:
....
Finished:
....
Source:
....

Why i read it:
....
....
....

It inspired me to:
....
....
....

Rating:

1 2 3 4 5

Ease of reading

1 2 3 4 5

☹ 😐 🙂

45

Started:

....

Finished:

....

Source:

....

Why i read it:

....
....
....

It inspired me to:

....
....
....

Rating:

1   2   3   4   5

Ease of reading

1   2   3   4   5

☹   😐   🙂

Title:

Author: ....

Subject: .... **Genre:** ....

Page count: .... **Pub date:** ....

Poperback ☐   e-book ☐   audiobook ☐

Fiction ☐   non fiction ☐

My review: ....
....
....
....
....
....
....
....
....
....
....
....
....
....
....

Quote from this book:

Title:

Author: ....

Subject: .... Genre: ....

Page count: .... Pub date: ....

Poperback ☐   e-book ☐   audiobook ☐

Fiction ☐   non fiction ☐

My review: ....
....
....
....
....
....
....
....
....
....
....
....
....
....
....

Quote from this book:

Started:
....

Finished:
....

Source:
....

Why i read it:
....
....
....

It inspired me to:
....
....
....

Rating:

1 2 3 4 5

Ease of reading

1 2 3 4 5

☹ 😐 🙂

47

Title:

Started:

....

Finished:

....

Source:

....

Why i read it:

....
....
....

It inspired me to:

....
....
....

Rating:

1 2 3 4 5

Ease of reading

1 2 3 4 5

☹ 😐 🙂

Author: ....

Subject: .... **Genre:** ....

Page count: .... **Pub date:** ....

Poperback ☐   e-book ☐   audiobook ☐

Fiction ☐   non fiction ☐

My review: ....
....
....
....
....
....
....
....
....
....
....
....
....
....
....
....
....

Quote from this book:

Title:

48

Author: ....

Subject: .... Genre: ....

Page count: .... Pub date: ....

Paperback ☐   e-book ☐   audiobook ☐

Fiction ☐   non fiction ☐

My review: ....
....
....
....
....
....
....
....
....
....
....
....
....
....
....

Quote from this book:

Started:
....

Finished:
....

Source:
....

Why i read it:
....
....
....

It inspired me to:
....
....
....

Rating:

1   2   3   4   5

Ease of reading

1   2   3   4   5

☹   😐   🙂

49

Title:

Started:
....

Finished:
....

Source:
....

Author: ....

Subject: .... **Genre:** ....

Page count: .... **Pub date:** ....

Poperback ☐   e-book ☐   audiobook ☐

Fiction ☐   non fiction ☐

Why i read it:
....
....
....

It inspired me to:
....
....
....

My review: ....
....
....
....
....
....
....
....
....
....
....
....
....
....
....
....
....

Rating:

1 2 3 4 5

Ease of reading

1 2 3 4 5

☹ 😐 🙂

Quote from this book:

Title:

50

Author: ....

Subject: .... Genre: ....

Page count: .... Pub date: ....

Poperback ☐   e-book ☐   audiobook ☐

Fiction ☐   non fiction ☐

My review: ....
....
....
....
....
....
....
....
....
....
....
....
....
....

Quote from this book:

Started:

....

Finished:

....

Source:

....

Why i read it:
....
....
....

It inspired me to:
....
....
....

Rating:

1   2   3   4   5

Ease of reading

1   2   3   4   5

☹   😐   🙂

51

Started:

....

Finished:

....

Source:

....

Why i read it:

....

....

....

It inspired me to:

....

....

....

Rating:

1 2 3 4 5

Ease of reading

1 2 3 4 5

☹ 😐 🙂

Title:

Author: ....

Subject: .... **Genre:** ....

Page count: .... **Pub date:** ....

Poperback ☐   e-book ☐   audiobook ☐

Fiction ☐   non fiction ☐

My review: ....

....

....

....

....

....

....

....

....

....

....

....

....

....

....

....

Quote from this book:

Title:

52

Author: ....

Subject: .... Genre: ....

Page count: .... Pub date: ....

Paperback ☐   e-book ☐   audiobook ☐

Fiction ☐   non fiction ☐

My review: ....
....
....
....
....
....
....
....
....
....
....
....
....
....
....
....

Quote from this book:

Started:

....

Finished:

....

Source:

....

Why i read it:

....
....
....

It inspired me to:

....
....
....

Rating:

1   2   3   4   5

Ease of reading

1   2   3   4   5

☹   😐   🙂

53

Started:

....

Finished:

....

Source:

....

Why i read it:

....
....
....

It inspired me to:

....
....
....

Rating:

1   2   3   4   5

Ease of reading

1   2   3   4   5

😞   😐   🙂

Title:

Author: ....

Subject: .... **Genre:** ....

Page count: .... **Pub date:** ....

Poperback ☐   e-book ☐   audiobook ☐

Fiction ☐   non fiction ☐

My review: ....
....
....
....
....
....
....
....
....
....
....
....
....
....
....
....
....

Quote from this book:

Title:

54

Author: ....

Subject: .... **Genre:** ....

Page count: .... **Pub date:** ....

Poperback ☐   e-book ☐   audiobook ☐

Fiction ☐   non fiction ☐

My review: ....
....
....
....
....
....
....
....
....
....
....
....
....
....
....

Quote from this book:

Started:
....

Finished:
....

Source:
....

Why i read it:
....
....
....

It inspired me to:
....
....
....

Rating:

1   2   3   4   5

Ease of reading

1   2   3   4   5

:(:| :)

55

Started:

....

Finished:

....

Source:

....

Why i read it:

....

....

....

It inspired me to:

....

....

....

Rating:

1 2 3 4 5

Ease of reading

1 2 3 4 5

😞   😐   🙂

Title:

Author: ....

Subject: .... **Genre:** ....

Page count: .... **Pub date:** ....

Poperback ☐   e-book ☐   audiobook ☐

Fiction ☐   non fiction ☐

My review: ....

....

....

....

....

....

....

....

....

....

....

....

....

....

....

....

Quote from this book:

Title:

56

Author: ....

Subject: .... Genre: ....

Page count: .... Pub date: ....

Poperback ☐   e-book ☐   audiobook ☐

Fiction ☐   non fiction ☐

Started:
....

Finished:
....

Source:
....

My review: ....
....
....
....
....
....
....
....
....
....
....
....
....
....

Why i read it:
....
....
....

It inspired me to:
....
....
....

Rating:

1   2   3   4   5

Ease of reading

1   2   3   4   5

Quote from this book:

57

Started:

Finished:

Source:

Why i read it:

It inspired me to:

Rating:

1 2 3 4 5

Ease of reading

1 2 3 4 5

Title:

Author:

Subject: Genre:

Page count: Pub date:

Poperback ☐ e-book ☐ audiobook ☐

Fiction ☐ non fiction ☐

My review:

Quote from this book:

Title:

58

Author: ....

Subject: .... Genre: ....

Page count: .... Pub date: ....

Poperback ☐   e-book ☐   audiobook ☐

Fiction ☐   non fiction ☐

My review: ....

....

....

....

....

....

....

....

....

....

....

....

....

....

....

Quote from this book:

Started:
....

Finished:
....

Source:

....

Why i read it:
....
....

It inspired me to:
....
....
....

Rating:

1   2   3   4   5

Ease of reading

1   2   3   4   5

☹   😐   🙂

59

Started:

....

Finished:

....

Source:

....

Why i read it:

....
....
....

It inspired me to:

....
....
....

Rating:

1 2 3 4 5

Ease of reading

1 2 3 4 5

☹ 😐 🙂

Title:

Author: ....

Subject: .... **Genre:** ....

Page count: .... **Pub date:** ....

Poperback ☐   e-book ☐   audiobook ☐

Fiction ☐   non fiction ☐

My review: ....
....
....
....
....
....
....
....
....
....
....
....
....
....
....

Quote from this book:

Title:

60

Author: ....

Subject: .... **Genre:** ....

Page count: .... **Pub date:** ....

Poperback ☐   **e-book** ☐   **audiobook** ☐

Fiction ☐   **non fiction** ☐

My review: ....
....
....
....
....
....
....
....
....
....
....
....
....
....
....

Quote from this book:

Started:
....

Finished:
....

Source:
....

Why i read it:
....
....

It inspired me to:
....
....
....

Rating:

1   2   3   4   5

Ease of reading

1   2   3   4   5

☹   😐   🙂

61

Started:

....

Finished:

....

Source:

....

Why i read it:

....
....
....

It inspired me to:

....
....
....

Rating:

1 2 3 4 5

Ease of reading

1 2 3 4 5

☹ 😐 🙂

Title:

Author: ....

Subject: .... **Genre:** ....

Page count: .... **Pub date:** ....

Poperback ☐   e-book ☐   audiobook ☐

Fiction ☐   non fiction ☐

My review: ....
....
....
....
....
....
....
....
....
....
....
....
....
....
....
....

Quote from this book:

Title:

62

Author: ....

Subject: .... Genre: ....

Page count: .... Pub date: ....

Paperback ☐   e-book ☐   audiobook ☐

Fiction ☐   non fiction ☐

My review: ....
....
....
....
....
....
....
....
....
....
....
....
....
....

Quote from this book:

Started:
....

Finished:
....

Source:
....

Why i read it:
....
....
....

It inspired me to:
....
....
....

Rating:

1 2 3 4 5

Ease of reading

1 2 3 4 5

☹ 😐 🙂

63

Started:

....

Finished:

....

Source:

....

Why i read it:

....
....
....

It inspired me to:

....
....
....

Rating:

1 2 3 4 5

Ease of reading

1 2 3 4 5

☹ 😐 🙂

Title:

Author: ....

Subject: .... **Genre:** ....

Page count: .... **Pub date:** ....

Poperback ☐   e-book ☐   audiobook ☐

Fiction ☐   non fiction ☐

My review: ....
....
....
....
....
....
....
....
....
....
....
....
....
....
....
....

Quote from this book:

Title:

64

Author: ....

Started:
....

Subject: .... Genre: ....

Finished:
....

Page count: .... Pub date: ....

Source:

Poperback ☐   e-book ☐   audiobook ☐

Fiction ☐   non fiction ☐

....

My review: ....
....
....
....
....
....
....
....
....
....
....
....
....
....
....
....
....

Why i read it:
....
....
....

It inspired me to:
....
....
....

Rating:

1   2   3   4   5

Ease of reading

1   2   3   4   5

☹   😐   🙂

Quote from this book:

65

Started:

....

Finished:

....

Source:

....

Why i read it:

....
....
....

It inspired me to:

....
....
....

Rating:

1 2 3 4 5

Ease of reading

1 2 3 4 5

☹ 😐 🙂

Title:

Author: ....

Subject: .... **Genre:** ....

Page count: .... **Pub date:** ....

Poperback ☐   e-book ☐   audiobook ☐

Fiction ☐   non fiction ☐

My review: ....
....
....
....
....
....
....
....
....
....
....
....
....
....
....
....
....

Quote from this book:

Title:

66

Author: ....

Subject: .... Genre: ....

Page count: .... Pub date: ....

Poperback ☐ e-book ☐ audiobook ☐

Fiction ☐ non fiction ☐

My review: ....
....
....
....
....
....
....
....
....
....
....
....
....
....
....
....
....

Quote from this book:

Started:

....

Finished:

....

Source:

....

Why i read it.
....
....
....

It inspired me to:
....
....
....

Rating:

1 2 3 4 5

Ease of reading

1 2 3 4 5

☹ 😐 🙂

67

Started:
....

Finished:

....

Source:

....

Why i read it:
....
....
....

It inspired me to:
....
....
....

Rating:

1   2   3   4   5

Ease of reading

1   2   3   4   5

Title:

Author: ....

Subject: .... **Genre:** ....

Page count: .... **Pub date:** ....

Poperback ☐   e-book ☐   audiobook ☐

Fiction ☐   non fiction ☐

My review: ....
....
....
....
....
....
....
....
....
....
....
....
....
....
....
....
....

Quote from this book:

Title:

68

Author: ....

Subject: .... **Genre:** ....

Page count: .... **Pub date:** ....

Poperback ☐   e-book ☐   audiobook ☐

Fiction ☐   non fiction ☐

Started:

....

Finished:

....

Source:

....

My review: ....
....
....
....
....
....
....
....
....
....
....
....
....
....

Why i read it:

....
....
....

It inspired me to:

....
....
....

Rating:

1   2   3   4   5

Ease of reading

1   2   3   4   5

😞   😐   🙂

Quote from this book:

69

Started:

....

Finished:

....

Source:

....

Why i read it:

....
....
....

It inspired me to:

....
....
....

Rating:

1 2 3 4 5

Ease of reading

1 2 3 4 5

😞 😐 🙂

Title:

Author: ....

Subject: .... **Genre:** ....

Page count: .... **Pub date:** ....

Poperback ☐   e-book ☐   audiobook ☐

Fiction ☐   non fiction ☐

My review: ....
....
....
....
....
....
....
....
....
....
....
....
....
....
....
....

Quote from this book:

Title:

Author: ....

Subject: ....   Genre: ....

Page count: ....   Pub date: ....

Poperback ☐   e-book ☐   audiobook ☐

Fiction ☐   non fiction ☐

My review: ....
....
....
....
....
....
....
....
....
....
....
....
....
....
....
....

Quote from this book:

Started:

....

Finished:

....

Source:

....

Why i read it:

....
....
....

It inspired me to:

....
....
....

Rating:

1   2   3   4   5

Ease of reading

1   2   3   4   5

☹   😐   🙂

71

Started:

....

Finished:

....

Source:

....

Why i read it:

....
....
....

It inspired me to:

....
....
....

Rating:

1　2　3　4　5

Ease of reading

1　2　3　4　5

☹　😐　🙂

Title:

Author: ....

Subject: .... **Genre:** ....

Page count: .... **Pub date:** ....

Poperback ☐　　e-book ☐　　audiobook ☐

Fiction ☐　　non fiction ☐

My review: ....
....
....
....
....
....
....
....
....
....
....
....
....
....
....
....

Quote from this book:

Title:

72

Author: ....

Subject: .... Genre: ....

Page count: .... Pub date: ....

Paperback ☐   e-book ☐   audiobook ☐

Fiction ☐   non fiction ☐

My review: ....
....
....
....
....
....
....
....
....
....
....
....
....
....
....
....

Quote from this book:

Started:

....

Finished:

....

Source:

....

Why i read it:
....
....
....

It inspired me to:
....
....
....

Rating:

1   2   3   4   5

Ease of reading

1   2   3   4   5

:(:| :)

73

Title:

Started:

Finished:

Source:

Why i read it:

It inspired me to:

Rating:

1 2 3 4 5

Ease of reading

1 2 3 4 5

Author:

Subject: Genre:

Page count: Pub date:

Poperback ☐   e-book ☐   audiobook ☐

Fiction ☐   non fiction ☐

My review:

Quote from this book:

Title:

Author: ....

Subject: .... Genre: ....

Page count: .... Pub date: ....

Poperback ☐   e-book ☐   audiobook ☐

Fiction ☐   non fiction ☐

My review: ....
....
....
....
....
....
....
....
....
....
....
....
....
....
....

Quote from this book:

Started:

....

Finished:

....

Source:

....

Why i read it:

....
....
....

It inspired me to:

....
....
....

Rating:

1   2   3   4   5

Ease of reading

1   2   3   4   5

☹   😐   🙂

75

Started:

....

Finished:

....

Source:

....

Why i read it:

....
....
....

It inspired me to:

....
....
....

Rating:

1 2 3 4 5

Ease of reading

1 2 3 4 5

☹ 😐 🙂

Title:

Author: ....

Subject: .... **Genre:** ....

Page count: .... **Pub date:** ....

Poperback ☐   **e-book** ☐   **audiobook** ☐

Fiction ☐   **non fiction** ☐

My review: ....
....
....
....
....
....
....
....
....
....
....
....
....
....
....
....

Quote from this book:

Title:

Author: ....

Subject: .... Genre: ....

Page count: .... Pub date: ....

Poperback ☐   e-book ☐   audiobook ☐

Fiction ☐   non fiction ☐

My review: ....
....
....
....
....
....
....
....
....
....
....
....
....
....
....
....

Quote from this book:

Started:
....

Finished:
....

Source:
....

Why i read it:
....
....
....

It inspired me to:
....
....
....

Rating:

1   2   3   4   5

Ease of reading

1   2   3   4   5

😞   😐   🙂

77

Title:

Started:

Finished:

Source:

Author: ....

Subject: .... Genre: ....

Page count: .... Pub date: ....

Poperback ☐   e-book ☐   audiobook ☐

Fiction ☐   non fiction ☐

Why i read it:
....
....
....

It inspired me to:
....
....
....

My review: ....
....
....
....
....
....
....
....
....
....
....
....
....
....
....
....
....

Rating:

1 2 3 4 5

Ease of reading

1 2 3 4 5

Quote from this book:

Title:

Author: ....

Subject: .... Genre: ....

Page count: .... Pub date: ....

Poperback ☐   e-book ☐   audiobook ☐

Fiction ☐   non fiction ☐

My review: ....
....
....
....
....
....
....
....
....
....
....
....
....
....
....

Quote from this book:

Started:

....

Finished:

....

Source:

....

Why i read it:

....
....
....

It inspired me to:

....
....
....

Rating:

1   2   3   4   5

Ease of reading

1   2   3   4   5

☹   😐   🙂

79

Started:

....

Finished:

....

Source:

....

Why i read it:

....
....
....

It inspired me to:

....
....
....

Rating:

1 2 3 4 5

Ease of reading

1 2 3 4 5

☹ 😐 🙂

Title:

Author: ....

Subject: .... **Genre:** ....

Page count: .... **Pub date:** ....

Poperback ☐   e-book ☐   audiobook ☐

Fiction ☐   non fiction ☐

My review: ....
....
....
....
....
....
....
....
....
....
....
....
....
....
....
....

Quote from this book:

Title:

80

Author: ....

Subject: .... **Genre:** ....

Page count: .... **Pub date:** ....

Poperback ☐   e-book ☐   audiobook ☐

Fiction ☐   non fiction ☐

Started:

....

Finished:

....

Source:

....

My review: ....
....
....
....
....
....
....
....
....
....
....
....
....
....

Why i read it:
....
....
....

It inspired me to:
....
....
....

Rating:

1 2 3 4 5

Ease of reading

1 2 3 4 5

☹ 😐 🙂

Quote from this book:

81

Started:

....

Finished:

....

Source:

....

Why i read it:

....
....
....

It inspired me to:

....
....
....

Rating:

1 2 3 4 5

Ease of reading

1 2 3 4 5

☹ 😐 🙂

Title:

Author: ....

Subject: .... **Genre:** ....

Page count: .... **Pub date:** ....

Poperback ☐   e-book ☐   audiobook ☐

Fiction ☐   non fiction ☐

My review: ....
....
....
....
....
....
....
....
....
....
....
....
....
....
....
....
....

Quote from this book:

Title:

82

Author: ....

Subject: .... Genre: ....

Page count: .... Pub date: ....

Poperback ☐   e-book ☐   audiobook ☐

Fiction ☐   non fiction ☐

My review: ....
....
....
....
....
....
....
....
....
....
....
....
....
....
....

Quote from this book:

Started:

....

Finished:

....

Source:

....

Why i read it:
....
....
....

It inspired me to:
....
....
....

Rating:

1 2 3 4 5

Ease of reading

1 2 3 4 5

😦 😐 🙂

83

Title:

Started:

....

Finished:

....

Source:

....

Author: ....

Subject: .... Genre: ....

Page count: .... Pub date: ....

Poperback ☐   e-book ☐   audiobook ☐

Fiction ☐   non fiction ☐

Why i read it:

....

....

....

It inspired me to:

....

....

....

My review: ....

....

....

....

....

....

....

....

....

....

....

....

....

....

....

....

Rating:

1 2 3 4 5

Ease of reading

1 2 3 4 5

☹   😐   🙂

Quote from this book:

Title:

84

Author: ....

Subject: .... Genre: ....

Page count: .... Pub date: ....

Poperback ☐   e-book ☐   audiobook ☐

Fiction ☐   non fiction ☐

My review: ....
....
....
....
....
....
....
....
....
....
....
....
....
....

Quote from this book:

Started:
....

Finished:
....

Source:
....

Why i read it:
....
....
....

It inspired me to:
....
....
....

Rating:

1 2 3 4 5

Ease of reading

1 2 3 4 5

☹ 😐 🙂

85

Started:

....

Finished:

....

Source:

....

Why i read it:

....
....
....

It inspired me to:

....
....
....

Rating:

1   2   3   4   5

Ease of reading

1   2   3   4   5

😞   😐   🙂

Title:

Author: ....

Subject: .... **Genre:** ....

Page count: .... **Pub date:** ....

Poperback ☐   e-book ☐   audiobook ☐

Fiction ☐   non fiction ☐

My review: ....
....
....
....
....
....
....
....
....
....
....
....
....
....
....
....

Quote from this book:

Title:

86

Author: ....

Subject: .... Genre: ....

Page count: .... Pub date: ....

Paperback ☐　　e-book ☐　　audiobook ☐

　　　Fiction ☐　　non fiction ☐

My review: ....
....
....
....
....
....
....
....
....
....
....
....
....
....
....

Quote from this book:

Started:
....

Finished:
....

Source:
....

Why i read it.
....
....
....

It inspired me to:
....
....
....

Rating:

1　2　3　4　5

Ease of reading

1　2　3　4　5

☹　😐　🙂

87

Started:
....

Finished:
....

Source:
....

Why i read it:
....
....
....

It inspired me to:
....
....
....

Rating:

1 2 3 4 5

Ease of reading

1 2 3 4 5

Title:

Author: ....

Subject: .... Genre: ....

Page count: .... Pub date: ....

Poperback ☐   e-book ☐   audiobook ☐

Fiction ☐   non fiction ☐

My review: ....
....
....
....
....
....
....
....
....
....
....
....
....
....
....
....

Quote from this book:

Title:

Author: ....

Subject: .... Genre: ....

Page count: .... Pub date: ....

Poperback ☐   e-book ☐   audiobook ☐

Fiction ☐   non fiction ☐

My review: ....
....
....
....
....
....
....
....
....
....
....
....
....
....
....

Quote from this book:

Started:

....

Finished:

....

Source:

....

Why i read it.

....
....
....

It inspired me to:

....
....
....

Rating:

1   2   3   4   5

Ease of reading

1   2   3   4   5

☹   😐   🙂

89

Started:

....

Finished:

....

Source:

....

Why i read it:

....
....
....

It inspired me to:

....
....
....

Rating:

1   2   3   4   5

Ease of reading

1   2   3   4   5

☹   😐   🙂

Title:

Author: ....

Subject: .... **Genre:** ....

Page count: .... **Pub date:** ....

Poperback ☐   e-book ☐   audiobook ☐

Fiction ☐   non fiction ☐

My review: ....
....
....
....
....
....
....
....
....
....
....
....
....
....
....
....
....

Quote from this book:

Title:

90

Author: ....

Subject: .... Genre: ....

Page count: .... Pub date: ....

Poperback ☐   e-book ☐   audiobook ☐

Fiction ☐   non fiction ☐

My review: ....
....
....
....
....
....
....
....
....
....
....
....
....
....
....

Quote from this book:

Started:
....

Finished:
....

Source:

....

Why i read it.
....
....
....

It inspired me to:
....
....
....

Rating:

1   2   3   4   5

Ease of reading

1   2   3   4   5

☹   😐   🙂

91

Started:

....

Finished:

....

Source:

....

Why i read it:

....
....
....

It inspired me to:

....
....
....

Rating:

1 2 3 4 5

Ease of reading

1 2 3 4 5

😞   😐   🙂

Title:

Author: ....

Subject:........................... **Genre:** ....

Page count:....................... **Pub date:** ....

Poperback ☐   e-book ☐   audiobook ☐

Fiction ☐   non fiction ☐

My review:..
....
....
....
....
....
....
....
....
....
....
....
....
....
....
....
....

Quote from this book:

Title:

Author: ....

Subject: .... Genre: ....

Page count: .... Pub date: ....

Poperback ☐   e-book ☐   audiobook ☐

Fiction ☐   non fiction ☐

My review: ....
....
....
....
....
....
....
....
....
....
....
....
....
....
....
....

Quote from this book:

Started:
....

Finished:
....

Source:
....

Why i read it:
....
....

It inspired me to:
....
....

Rating:

1 2 3 4 5

Ease of reading

1 2 3 4 5

☹ 😐 🙂

93

Started:

....

Finished:

....

Source:

....

Why i read it:

....
....
....

It inspired me to:

....
....
....

Rating:

1 2 3 4 5

Ease of reading

1 2 3 4 5

☹ 😐 🙂

Title:

Author: ....

Subject: .... **Genre:** ....

Page count: .... **Pub date:** ....

Poperback ☐   e-book ☐   audiobook ☐

Fiction ☐   non fiction ☐

My review: ....
....
....
....
....
....
....
....
....
....
....
....
....
....
....
....

Quote from this book:

Title:

Author: ....

Subject: .... Genre: ....

Page count: .... Pub date: ....

Poperback ☐   e-book ☐   audiobook ☐

Fiction ☐   non fiction ☐

My review: ....
....
....
....
....
....
....
....
....
....
....
....
....
....
....

Quote from this book:

Started:

....

Finished:

....

Source:

....

Why i read it.

....
....
....

It inspired me to:

....
....
....

Rating:

1   2   3   4   5

Ease of reading

1   2   3   4   5

☹   😐   🙂

95

Started:

....

Finished:

....

Source:

....

Why i read it:

....
....
....

It inspired me to:

....
....
....

Rating:

1 2 3 4 5

Ease of reading

1 2 3 4 5

😟   😐   🙂

Title:

Author: ....

Subject: .... **Genre:** ....

Page count: .... **Pub date:** ....

Poperback ☐   e-book ☐   audiobook ☐

Fiction ☐   non fiction ☐

My review: ....
....
....
....
....
....
....
....
....
....
....
....
....
....
....
....
....
....

Quote from this book:

Title:

96

Author: ....

Subject: .... Genre: ....

Page count: .... Pub date: ....

Poperback ☐   e-book ☐   audiobook ☐

Fiction ☐   non fiction ☐

My review: ....
....
....
....
....
....
....
....
....
....
....
....
....
....

Quote from this book:

Started:
....

Finished:
....

Source:
....

Why i read it:
....
....
....

It inspired me to:
....
....
....

Rating:

1   2   3   4   5

Ease of reading

1   2   3   4   5

😞   😐   🙂

97

Started:

....

Finished:

....

Source:

....

Why i read it:

....
....
....

It inspired me to:

....
....
....

Rating:

1 2 3 4 5

Ease of reading

1 2 3 4 5

☹ 😐 🙂

Title:

Author: ....

Subject: .... **Genre:** ....

Page count: .... **Pub date:** ....

Poperback ☐   e-book ☐   audiobook ☐

Fiction ☐   non fiction ☐

My review: ....
....
....
....
....
....
....
....
....
....
....
....
....
....
....
....
....

Quote from this book:

Title:

Author:

Subject: Genre:

Page count: Pub date:

Poperback ☐   e-book ☐   audiobook ☐

Fiction ☐   non fiction ☐

My review:

Quote from this book:

Started:

Finished:

Source:

Why i read it:

It inspired me to:

Rating:

1   2   3   4   5

Ease of reading

1   2   3   4   5

☹   😐   🙂

99

Started:

....

Finished:

....

Source:

....

Why i read it:

....
....
....

It inspired me to:

....
....
....

Rating:

1 2 3 4 5

Ease of reading

1 2 3 4 5

☹ 😐 🙂

Title:

Author: ....

Subject: .... **Genre:** ....

Page count: .... **Pub date:** ....

Poperback ☐   e-book ☐   audiobook ☐

Fiction ☐   non fiction ☐

My review: ....
....
....
....
....
....
....
....
....
....
....
....
....
....
....
....

Quote from this book:

Title:

100

Author: ....

Subject: .... Genre: ....

Page count: .... Pub date: ....

Poperback ☐   e-book ☐   audiobook ☐

Fiction ☐   non fiction ☐

My review: ....
....
....
....
....
....
....
....
....
....
....
....
....
....
....

Quote from this book:

Started:
....

Finished:
....

Source:

....

Why i read it.
....
....
....

It inspired me to:
....
....
....

Rating:

1 2 3 4 5

Ease of reading

1 2 3 4 5

☹ 😐 🙂

101

Started:

....

Finished:

....

Source:

....

Why i read it:

....
....
....

It inspired me to:

....
....
....

Rating:

1   2   3   4   5

Ease of reading

1   2   3   4   5

☹   😐   🙂

Title:

Author: ....

Subject: .... **Genre:** ....

Page count: .... **Pub date:** ....

Poperback ☐   e-book ☐   audiobook ☐

Fiction ☐   non fiction ☐

My review: ....
....
....
....
....
....
....
....
....
....
....
....
....
....
....
....
....

Quote from this book:

Title:

Author: ....

Subject: .... Genre: ....

Page count: .... Pub date: ....

Poperback ☐   e-book ☐   audiobook ☐

Fiction ☐   non fiction ☐

My review: ....
....
....
....
....
....
....
....
....
....
....
....
....
....
....

Quote from this book:

Started:

....

Finished:

....

Source:

....

Why i read it:

....
....
....

It inspired me to:

....
....
....

Rating:

1 2 3 4 5

Ease of reading

1 2 3 4 5

☹ 😐 🙂

103

Started:

....

Finished:

....

Source:

....

Why i read it:

....
....
....

It inspired me to:

....
....
....

Rating:

1 2 3 4 5

Ease of reading

1 2 3 4 5

☹ 😐 🙂

Title:

Author: ....

Subject: .... **Genre:** ....

Page count: .... **Pub date:** ....

Poperback ☐   e-book ☐   audiobook ☐

Fiction ☐   non fiction ☐

My review: ....
....
....
....
....
....
....
....
....
....
....
....
....
....
....
....

Quote from this book:

Title:

Author: ....

Subject: .... Genre: ....

Page count: .... Pub date: ....

Poperback ☐   e-book ☐   audiobook ☐

Fiction ☐   non fiction ☐

My review: ....
....
....
....
....
....
....
....
....
....
....
....
....
....

Quote from this book:

Started:
....

Finished:
....

Source:
....

Why i read it:
....
....

It inspired me to:
....
....
....

Rating:

1   2   3   4   5

Ease of reading

1   2   3   4   5

My To Be Read List

Title: ....

Author: .... Date Added: ....

Why: ....

Title: ....

Author: .... Date Added: ....

Why: ....

Title: ....

Author: .... Date Added: ....

Why: ....

Title: ....

Author: .... Date Added: ....

Why: ....

Title: ....

Author: .... Date Added: ....

Why: ....

Title : ....

Author : .... Date Added : ....

Why : ....

Title : ....

Author : .... Date Added : ....

Why : ....

Title : ....

Author : .... Date Added : ....

Why : ....

Title : ....

Author : .... Date Added : ....

Why : ....

Title : ....

Author : .... Date Added : ....

Why : ....

Title : ....

Author : .... Date Added : ....

Why : ....

Title : ....

Author : .... Date Added : ....

Why : ....

Title : ....

Author : .... Date Added : ....

Why : ....

Title : ....

Author : .... Date Added : ....

Why : ....

Title : ....

Author : .... Date Added : ....

Why : ....

Title : ....

Author : .... Date Added : ....

Why : ....

Title : ....

Author : .... Date Added : ....

Why : ....

Title: ....

Author: .... Date Added: ....

Why: ....

Title: ....

Author: .... Date Added: ....

Why: ....

Title: ....

Author: .... Date Added: ....

Why: ....

Title: ....

Author: .... Date Added: ....

Why: ....

Title: ....

Author: .... Date Added: ....

Why: ....

Title: ....

Author: .... Date Added: ....

Why: ....

Title : ....

Author : .... Date Added : ....

Why : ....

Title : ....

Author : .... Date Added : ....

Why : ....

Title : ....

Author : .... Date Added : ....

Why : ....

Title : ....

Author : .... Date Added : ....

Why : ....

Title : ....

Author : .... Date Added : ....

Why : ....

Title : ....

Author : .... Date Added : ....

Why : ....

Title : ....

Author : .... Date Added : ....

Why : ....

Title : ....

Author : .... Date Added : ....

Why : ....

Title : ....

Author : .... Date Added : ....

Why : ....

Title : ....

Author : .... Date Added : ....

Why : ....

Title : ....

Author : .... Date Added : ....

Why : ....

Title : ....

Author : .... Date Added : ....

Why : ....

Title : ....

Author : .... Date Added : ....

Why : ....

Title : ....

Author : .... Date Added : ....

Why : ....

Title : ....

Author : .... Date Added : ....

Why : ....

Title : ....

Author : .... Date Added : ....

Why : ....

Title : ....

Author : .... Date Added : ....

Why : ....

Title : ....

Author : .... Date Added : ....

Why : ....

Just one more Chapter

Thank you!

We hope you enjoyed our book.

As a small family company, your feedback is very important to us .

Please let us know how you like our book at :

pickme.readme@gmail.com